SPECUL

Copl

ISBN: 978-1-913642-55-6

Cover design by Aaron Kent

Edited & typeset by Aaron Kent

Broken Sleep Books (2021)

Broken Sleep Books Ltd
Rhydwen,
Talgarreg,
SA44 4HB
Wales

Contents

Of two poems one sentimental and one not
I choose both.
- *Alice Notley, 'A Baby is Born out of a White Owl's Forehead'*

Yet one word more – grief boundeth where it falls,
Not with the empty hollowness, but weight
- *William Shakespeare, Richard II, Act 1 Scene 2*

Speculum

Hannah Copley

First

to the skinned kit,
to the hare alive
to the red, warm dark,
to the kidney whose
black fuzz rings the crown
of its soft boned ball,
to the white silk ribbon
of limb on the electric
screen, to the cauled
and darting marrow,
fern-fingered fox, digits
balled and then unfurled,
to the crystalizing glass

An archive

Named Extreme Cure, or, On the Misnomer
of the Term Heroic Medicine. There is a rolling stack

dedicated to the wax each child dons to face the crowned light.
Cabinets for all the coaxed substances: colostrum, milk, placenta,

the shed lining of a womb. A microfilm that discusses how blood
can cover a table and a floor without the presence of a blade.

One file records how pushing is its own emetic – during,
and later, gingerly, amidst a fractured tailbone and each raw wound.

There is a city of death certificates, with new tower blocks
built every year, and a room with an ancient projector that loops a film

on how the women used to midwife and do still. Thirty hours
of work produces forty-eight centimetres of bawling result;

of vellum skin tucked into its proper place. See in this file
this spooling marvel of vernix and flesh.

Juice

All through Tuesday the air smelled like one big orange slice

as if I could dip my fingers in the bedroom wall
and bring them back coated in syrup.

I could eat all the oranges I wanted:
I was twenty-one and home for the summer
and my dad was dead and love was oranges
and the dark red post-box
rusting on the corner of the street

and I was pregnant by mistake.

It was like I was sick and oranges were the cure.
Oranges and women's magazines with names like
Time for a Break and *Chat* that had spa day giveaways

next to headlines like Drugged and Raped
by Jack the Ripper's Ghost! and Married to my Mother!

and My Amazing Sex…with a Wall!

that I could skim while I pressed my thumb nail
into another orange globe. I didn't even need to look up

to make a hole big enough to suck out all the juice.

I could just put my mouth to the rind and keep going
until there was nothing left inside.

Speculum

According to James Marion Sims, "Father of Modern Gynaecology",
who wrote his life story in the imaginatively named *The Story
of My Life*, when another physician heard that he was heading
to doctor the Westcott plantation, he remarked:

> 'you had better take
> your instruments along with you,
> for you may want to use them'.

Let's place all the emphasis on the *want*,
given how quietly terrifying it is. *Murder,*

She Wrote is on the tv again and there has been
a gruesome death at the beach, but luckily
Jessica thought to pack rubber gloves, measuring
tape, notebook, pen and a Dictaphone
in her bag.

Teeth

The listicle, Fifteen Disgusting Facts About Your Body,
includes an x-ray of a baby's skull, complete

with milk teeth stacked up like jaunty tower blocks
inside the bone holes. Did You Know,

says number nine of the listicle, that women
are born with all the eggs they will ever own?

It's exhilarating to know what I'm capable of
shrugging off, how every minute is an act of giving.

The other women in the clinic look like they've given
up their bones and muscles too.

We lay in our recliners like dead dolls. None of us
knows how to transcend tenderness yet

and when it's time to go home, I look down
and see I haven't got my shoes on.

Anarcha is a window and a door in the air

Problem (1) is one of naming:

As in, there is a misspelled first name in this census record,
and nothing else

Here is another woman
with eclampsia on page two of the document.

Here she is dead in a footnote.

Here we all are clattering together like lost keys in a tin.
Pick one of us to get nowhere.

Haworth, 1855

'Martha tenderly waited on her mistress, and from time to time tried to cheer her with the thought of the baby that was coming. "I dare say I shall be glad sometime," she would say; "but I am so ill – so weary" Then she took to her bed, too weak to sit up ... Long days and longer nights went by; still the same relentless nausea and faintness.'
  - Elizabeth Gaskell

It was there already, yes,
in those bone cold classrooms,
in the chants of *homo, hominis, homini*
drifting out between the iron bars.

But this is different. This is slow,
this is fragile. This is all sighs and rustlings,
retching and sobs. Loneliness,
I now know, is guttural.

I dare say I'll be glad
when it's over, but as it is I feel like
I've been cleaved. Stomach, lungs, throat
frayed like a caught seam,

mind spooling on the floor.
Under night's cloak, beds slip
their posts, sheets tie themselves in knots,
pillows calcify and crumble to a fine dust.

I wake each morning hot, threadbare,
my linen twisted, this makeshift body
kept in place by the smallest dart of nerve,
this makeshift heart still in my ear.

I dare say though, that I'll be lighter
in a month, but in my throat
there's a bitterness that will not shift.
My teeth are bird's eggs crunching

under coach wheels, my tongue
is torn cocoons on garden lawns, my lips
the dull skin of a cobra coiled behind
museum glass. But I shall be glad

sometime, I'll forget the smell
of an egg yolk, the slimy warmth of butter
as it runs across my tongue. I'll want
other things than unripe plums

and blackberries green and hard as stone,
In two months I'll see the white heather,
the dappled breasts of merlin, sheldapple.
My eyes will catch the winchat flushed

and bolting from its thicket bed.
In a year, I'll feel the backwards pull
of a skirt hem through tangled gorse,
the sharp embrace of a bramble hedge.

As I lie here soft and raw as dough,
I know tomorrow will prove infinitely
brighter. Even now, I can almost feel
your uncut letter in my hand.

Speculum [2]

Problem (2) is one of metaphor.
What is the appropriateness of fistula
to describe the hole in the archive
between the body of writing and the body of the patient?

Follow the sign for the tunnel between
the perfected gynaecological procedure
and the agony of the bondswoman whose vagina
is repeatedly penetrated by the curved end of the spoon.

This is a test. Perhaps only the description of the act itself,
as in, I am free enough to ball up my writing hand,
and tear my way to sympathy. Sonnet as hand-

crafted speculum tried and tried again;
as curved needle and gauze. Here I am placing fingers
in other people's wounds; here I am wounding.

'Building a little hospital'

Doctor says *the women are clamouring for it.*

Doctor reassures us that they do not feel it
like our wives and daughters would.

We are testing our delicacies here. Or rather,
they tested theirs so that we don't have to.

[The *Sims Position (fig. 1)* involves the subject climbing
naked onto the operating table. On all fours, her legs
parted, she is physically restrained for the duration of
the experiment by two white male assistants, who
hold her thighs and arms].

                              Doctor chides
that only delicate middle-class women can afford the time
to cultivate disorders like extreme morning sickness
and postnatal depression.

Doctor says, *she agreed without any prompting.*

After two years even the assistants quit.

Child

[Sims Farm, Federal Census, Montgomery Ward, December 5, 1850.
List of occupants: Twelve female slaves;
five male child slaves; one mulatto girl, aged one]

We remind ourselves again and again
that there is no such thing
as a first encounter.

Fourth, fifth, sixth generation

Record be half-damned. There is no box
for fictive kin, for othermothers,
for each shadow
child born and nursed

between four women, for bonds
as sweet and tightly spun
as sugar.

Polish Aubade

for Stanislawa Leszczyńska 1896-1974.

To never wish
  through two

Polish winters
  for morning

is astounding.
  But then, why

would anyone
  when it arrives

in black boots.
  And why would

anyone when
  it only speaks

in numbers
  and why would

anyone when it
  brings the barrel

to drown them.
  There are so few

ways to be unruly
  when there are

no rules, but better
  frost lit black

than an iron-
  wrapped sun.

You say later
  that when

the second gong
  sounds and

the lights
  are put out

you are free
  to watch

each icicle glimmer;
  you are free

to watch
  them shine

as a great crystal
chandelier in an

extinguished house.
  Sixty

no a hundred
  branches growing

through the roof.
  One for every five

patients to pull
  down and suck.

Better moonlight
  to lay kidney bowl

and scissors
  and your labour

out on the stove
  and work.

And when
  they come free

in the darkness
 you can wrap

them up in paper
 rag   and hand

and place them
 down onto

the quiet bodies
 that bore them

small ice cold
 unnumbered.

Hyperemesis Gravidarum

Ignore the Smirnoff Black balanced on a headstone   don't
take into account the whisky in a water bottle at lunchtime
labels can be picked off in longing   other people's butts get
re-born behind the garage   we're in the morning after the
night before and there is no water near the bed   and you
remember   the meat falling off the donner like a dress
    that *gluey pie*   all the wet throats   and it is *Dangerous
Liaisons: why syphilis   and gonorrhoea have returned to haunt
Britain*   while strangers push their tongues to the back of
your throat   the unwatered breath   but labels can be
picked off   in longing   don't sweat the muscular hollows
of your heart   or   a bad joke   and there's the saliva again
there's the raw pork in the pan   the foreskin facials on
Groupon   you chat briefly   to a co-worker
about water boarding before going back   to your desk
the school pays a visit to the abattoir   is it still
there rotting in the fridge   you're a yellow streak   of piss
the bin smell on a Thursday   and I'm   all nosegays
and chewing gum and ginger   and I'm going to brush
your teeth again   it is swilling   it is swallowing   it is
owning up   it is queasy   I'm practicing   all the words
like bilious   and viscera   and qualms   and burdens
for the smell of his body   because sometimes labels can be
picked off skin   it is his turn this time   it is your body
it is all in your belly   it is all in your womb   it is all in
your mind   it is all in your mouth.

A whole forest of cut trees

i. [Illustration from *The compleat midwife's companion: or, the art of midwifry improv'd. Directing child-bearing women how to order themselves in their conception, breeding, bearing, and nursing of children*, Mrs Jane Sharp, 1724]

In early illustration cliques, male bodies were always
the go-to cadavers. It was a seller's market you see, the seller
being the king, or the constable, or the gaoler, or the hangmen
or the criminal looking to make a killing.
You got whatever ration you could get and made it last.
There was also the matter of how useful a female cadaver
could actually be to the doctor, philosopher or barber surgeon,
it being almost as normal as the male body in all ways
except the breasts, the ovaries, the uterus
and the deviation within the opening.

ii. [Plate: XXXIII, A sett of anatomical tables, illustration by J.v. Rymsdyk, 1754]

Dr William Smellie, Lanark prodigy, ground-breaking *accoucheur*
of the mid-Eighteenth Century,
developer and promoter of the steel-lock [The 'Smellie lock'] forceps
and the curve and double curve forceps (tire-tête),
proud owner of a leather-lined manikin
with a functional vagina in his home study,
teacher, writer, 'a great horse godmother of a he-wife',
promoter of the natural birth, proficient of the violoncello,
the recorder, and the church organ,
a careful man by most accounts,
unfussy, kind, rescuer of the breech,
inflater of the punctured lung,
publishes *A Treatise on the Theory and Practice of Midwifery* and *A Sett
of Anatomical Tables, with Explanations, and an Abridgement, of the Practice
of Midwifery* in a great rush.
Here, for the first time, is a working atlas
of the pregnant female body. Thirty-nine plates,
drawn from life in red chalk by Jan van Rymsdyck and Peter Camper
-
a miracle of the printing press as well as the artist's hand.
We are close enough now to see our breath
hit the bodies in the cold room.
Here, in vivid detail, is a gravid uterus
rising like a balloon behind each severed thigh.
Here, for the first time, is a tiny head
with curled blonde hair forever stuck
as it travels down through the disembodied pelvis.
Here, rendered huge in close up, is a baby's arm
protruding from a truncated torso.
Here, complete with a smattering of pubic hair,
is an illustration of female genitalia.

iii. [Plate: front view of the pregnant uterus and pelvic area, showing the skin peeled away to reveal the swollen womb. Copperplate engraving by R. Strange after J.v. Rymsdyk, 1774]

It is 1754 and we are in a genitalia arms race.
William Hunter, East Kilbride boy,
pupil of Smellie, personal physician to Queen Charlotte,
accoucheur-about-town, finds a hole in the market
and fills it with flayed women.
The first edition of the Atlas is copper plated
and the roughly the same size height and width as a pillow.
Now we have cadavers in 3D.
Now we have cartilage and muscle
and huge faces squashed against wombs.
Here is failed childbirth in all its glory.
The Anatomy of the Human Gravid Uterus Exhibited in Figures
comes out in the same year as his mentor's Sett.
To create his USP, Hunter orders his plates
in reverse order - dead during labour
all the way down to dead at five weeks gone.
Male-midwives hail it as a marvel.

iv [Plate: dissection of the pregnant uterus, showing the foetus at nine months. Copperplate engraving by R. Strange after I.V. Rymsdyk, 1774]

No danger, then, of longing
      for this flayed intimacy,

for bone and tissue
wrought out

      in chalk the colour
of cherry wine.

Dismemberment
as the best line of defence
against caring too much.

It turns out the corpse's *I*
is as easy as a vestment

to tear away. I read

that John Clare lost his mind
when they maimed his trees -

turned common oak and poplar
to smooth-edged stump -
an ancient forest cut short at his shin.

The metal is waiting to serrate.

Give us the right tools and we can
create a whole history of rings
instead of trees.

Handheld mirror

How we laughed
when we realised that we'd mis-labelled
the labias;

had marked
Labia Majora as Labia Minora
on the cartoon diagram of external

female genitalia
in *The Guardian* online test. Two women
in their late twenties with doctorates

and mirrors and labias.
Point to the Urethra, directs the quiz,
as I stare at a sweet pie falling loose

from its crust.
Want to come star gazing tonight and see
the she-bear?

My partner
gets full marks; smug; can't understand how
two educated women don't know

their Labia Majoras
from their Labia Minoras. *Point to the Clitoris,*
demands the quiz. *Point to its hood.*

Person of the Year

[three hours]

I.M. Salomé Karwah. 1988 – 2017.

Ye   a'a   but   struggling to   you through the   [as
in partition - as in lover wrapped tight in a thin sheet – as in heavy
rains on tin] Stay   car, ma   m [as in passage – as in tin can
cracked earthen - as in any other jar to hold each piece of grief]
Don't   yourself [as in to fret is to be alive] Today is   day
for us   [as in the sound the road makes when it
melts] No, glass   necessary [as in water as in bread as in touch is
not] An absolute [as in there should be a thing other than
absolutes] No,   is   on call   [as real as you or I
or Jesus Christ barely an idea in the mind of his mother]
glove is esse   al [as a road is – as a light]   mask is
essential too [as a cracked tap is – as a wing shorn bird still flaps]
you can   I'm also hot [as the sun is sometimes burnt by
itself] But I can't   through all   glass [as in father in a
thin sheet in a burning box] No ma'am,   stay [as in I cannot
hold even the coil of a shed hair] Lie yourself   the
seats [as in a makeshift tent unfurls] No, don't roll it   [as
in the stink   of hazmat sweat – as in the human smell of rot]
I can't   it hurts   [as in bad womb stitch bad
split – bad mouth - as in how blood and spit don't know
themselves - as in bad scratch - as in odour as in wound - as in red
cross like the sun's own – as in each tethered spot of grief] Not
t   ching   essential [as in all absolute things are] you remain
import   us [as in feared – as in unmade – as in a living
object] plea   don't r   down   ndow [as in I will never
carry you   away from this place] There is no
   one

Pup

On Monday, Dr Fordyce forbad the child's having the breast, and we therefore procured puppies …'
– William Godwin, *Memoirs of the Author of 'A Vindication of the Rights of Woman' London, 1797*

I.

The house is breathing on its own again –
the kitchen door creaking on its hinges,
the hourly chime from the parlour shelf,
the tap of the old magnolia on the study glass –
for a while I thought it wouldn't make it,
not with all that sound drowning it.

Three days of the backwards and forwards
of front doors, footfall, muffled voices in the hall,
street noise stolen by the carpet,
blocked out by bolted windows,
then a gentle knock, and suddenly
the whole place was alive.

Urgent high-pitched yaps, and another wail
ringing through the house. I'd forgotten
that we weren't alone, or that such tiny innards
could make such a sound.
But never mind bodies, rooms.
What can they ever do but hold us.

II.

I spent three days with breasts sharper
than smashed stone. I was becoming diamond,
coal.

Even before she came I could squeeze the beestings
from my left nipple at the very thought.

Some knowledge leaks away so simply.

III.

First Mrs Blenkensop tried,
her big arms pink like boiled ham,
then the men, with their bag of tools.

Each took their turn to pull me apart
and all the time she just lay there,
milk drunk and napping on my chest.

IV.

I hear their claws on the landing first.

Two young King Charles Cavaliers.
Around their little necks they wear collars
the colour of quince, and one – the smallest –
pads across the bed with mud still in the creases of his paws.

I hadn't known they were coming.
Or maybe I did know
and didn't hold onto it, the way
you don't hold on to the sharp side of a knife.

When they latch, the points
of their teeth catch the skin.
No matter. There is blood already on the sheets.
As I stroke each little head, run each silky ear

between my finger and my thumb,
their fur feels as soft
as the down and blanket
of a baby girl.

As they settle on my chest
they are quiet, suckling, undoing every knot,
swallowing each stone. *Imagine her,*
Fordyce says,

but I can't remember if she even has a name.
I didn't get a chance to memorise
the proportions of the squashed and mottled face
as she lay pressed into my chest.

When I close my eyes all I can see
are dead roots, a forest of densely packed trees,
the purple cuts of a lung,
chopped up and piled upon a clean white plate.

I open my eyes and fix them on the cornice
in the top corner of the room. Beneath the coverlet
I can feel their little bodies shaking,
so precious and small.

File [1]

████████████ Born April 1905. Thin, pale, Presbyterian.

Marks and scars: a wine stain shaped like a shell
covering the left brow. Family: one
older brother: navy, two sisters
under five: chance of multiples. Mother:
deceased ('18. influenza). Father:
welder. Skills: laundry, cooking, keeping house.
Character: a good girl by all accounts.

The incident took place at the residence
of a family friend. Father: not named.

Belongings: one set of undergarments,
one cardigan, one dress, one pair of shoes
one teddy bear, one Bible (King James). Note:
no coat. Six months gone. Beginning to show.

File [2]

██████████████████ Born August 1907.
Minor. Originally from Cork.

Narrow pelvis. Underweight. Condition
visible. Deemed to be high risk. Thin arms
and legs. Pale. On close examination
clear signs of self-neglect. In need of iron,
clothing, guidance in matters pertaining
to personal hygiene. Eldest of six
(ages nine months, three, five, nine, and ten).

Mother: frail. Father: aware of situation
and consents to planned arrangement. Patient
refuses to discuss events that led
to her condition. Seven months gone.
Infant to be removed. Children's home informed.

Statue

Ann Lovett. 6 April 1968 – 31 January 1984. Granard, County Longford.

I haven't found a place to keep you safe yet
                              yet safety is the feeling I want
                                        for us also

also wanting warmth, a bath, a little bit of understanding
                              understanding only a bit of what
                              you were thinking

thinking of where you came to hide
                              as hidden things come back and
                                        then stay exposed

as exposure stays on a record of a person
                                        people change around
                              their exposed skin

skin exposed, legs parted
                    a part of a leg seen by boys on
                              their way home

home being another exposure,
                    erasure as a lack
                                        of back story

stories back and forth between parish
                              pariahs never allowed
          to stay safe

so I put you back for safe keeping behind
                              the statue, the line end
the space.

The Mother's Hospital, Clapton, Christmas Day, 1973.

for Nicholas

The card says CONFIDENTIAL, and THIS MUST BE KEPT SAFE
as if to take possession of the paper was enough.
'Single Mother', 'Minor', unfixed address. The rest is LMP,
EDC - a host of acronyms she's never learnt.

The walls are tinged in yellow. Fifteen beds, half filled,
with paper chains and cheap red foil draped across the gap
between each metal frame. A silver tinsel Christmas tree
sits on the nursing station and when the ward doors swing open
she can hear O Little Town of Bethlehem ring out
from the other room, where the choir of on-call doctors,
porters, nurses, harmonise with the married mothers.

Five miles away, in her own mother's house, Mahalia
sings out from the record player. O Holy Night, she cries,
O driving rain, O the traffic on the Clapton Road.
O the meter running as she roots around for a change of clothes.

When the nurses bring the newborns in she doesn't smile
or sing along. Turns her face away. Knows anyway
that her boy remains behind the glass to wail
with the others whose faces are too dark to be
the stand-in Messiah in the Hackney version
of their nativity play.

Five miles away, her mother sways. Fall on your knees
the music calls. She listens for her family's voices
in the yellow walls. O night divine, fifteen
and still waiting for a council flat. O the boy
who she has yet to hold. O the way she feels so small,
O the thin white legs of the only babygrow she owns.

Lost boys

"I can say that without fear of contraception".
Hylda Baker, *Nearest and Dearest*

At Brinsworth we do the cabaret
every other Wednesday. I'm wheeled in
for the 'stimulation' and the nurses say
give us one, Hylda, tell us another
even though they know. I've lost
them all. They've taken off and left me
like every other scoundrel in a pinstripe.
They were always so ready
to unzip, always so eager to leave.

Go on, the others heckle,
as if they could get up,
leering from their wheelchairs
like black-robed judges from the bench,
You know, Y' know, and the silence chimes
like a pin drop through my empty head.

I've lost enough lovers to fill
The Queen's Theatre twice through.
Some ran on foot, others sped away
in the Bentleys they were meant to chauffer,
their buffed hats left on the hallway table,
aftershave mingling with the others on the sheets.
Many simply couldn't keep up.
One tried to take my Cha-Cha with him
when he ran. All those lost Cynthias. All gone.

And I lost a child once, and then I lost another.
I kept them safe in all the wrong places,
mislaid them like keys hidden in a fireplace.
They were stones in a champagne flute,
I was always bound to smash.
But they were there for a while,
hanging on, two faceless punters waiting
for the gag, and then it all slipped out
of me as easily as a giggle. Once is a mistake.
Twice is careless. By the end of it
you could hear a pin drop in my heart.

History play

Forget, forgive, conclude and be agreed:
Our doctors say this is no time to bleed.
(Adjoa Andoh in William Shakespeare's, *Richard II*, Act 1 Scene 1)
The Sam Wanamaker Playhouse, 2019

Errata 1, or the misrepresentation of witchcraft

• Fresh blood smells
of iron and sugar.

• There was no hare
or bird or lamb flayed open,
no pigeon guts laid out to make
a blood brail on the stones.

• Explanation: it's too easy
to misread the purple tree
sagging in the open bowl.

Errata 2, or the properties of metal

For all the big words on constitution
you only have to tread across those slushed-through fields
to see how men's bodies are as soft as fontanelles.

Errata 3, or the Midwife as Archbishop

The top of each wet head
crowns itself through an open arch.

I watch, delighted, each coronation
as bloody as the last.

Denim

I had to lay down
in the changing room
and pull up the zip
with a clothes hanger
but when I came out
the shop assistant
smiled and said
they're perfect
and I smiled back
and said *they feel*
amazing and I paid
and walked out
of the shop
still fastened in
and two weeks later
{when I came apart}
in a Marks and Spencer's
multi-story car park
the blue seams held
together for the two
minutes it took
to hurry across
menswear shoes
and the food
court past the fresh
food counter
selling quiches
and the bunches
of orange and red
flowers near
the chocolates
and magazines
to the only room
that would accept
what I had come
to return and
while I walked
and did not look
at the other

people's faces
the emptiness
in my stomach
bloomed a black
flower for them
and the ligature came
loose and I knew
that soon they
would fit my hips
as if they had
been sewn with
just these bones
in mind

Ars poetica

Here intention and reality
can divide, multiply.
A straight-faced technician
tells you there is no heartbeat.

Your words are growing
in all the wrong places.
The words themselves
are all wrong.

There are no words after all.
You must go
into another room now
and get rid of your words.

Ghost therapist

You'll never be happy at the same time,
I hiss through the extractor fan.

Old desires grow up like grass
from the garden that contains

my dismembered corpse.
At any given moment

I am never *like* a ghost. I'm either
a ghost or I am just a voice

in the walls of your skull.
You could just change, I whisper

from inside the microwave
at the second before it pings.

Today, your baby is a beautiful knife.
Next week he'll be something else

to flay you. I can tell you all about it
if you'd listen.

The thin white candles
used to pray to the Virgin Mother;
a 105mm long bone stylet;
a crochet hook; marrow root
whittled into the shape of a spoon;
stagnant water rinsed through a lead pipe;
a lead pipe; an unspecified amount of wet
chalk plaster; a wood pestle; a wire hanger;
lying naked face-down in a snowbank;
gin; crouching in a hot bath to take up
the steam; visiting an aunt out of state;
a weekend trip to Liverpool; flying
down the stairs.

Games

16 June, 2016.

On other days I wake at six thirty and then snooze
with the alarm going off every five minutes until I give in
but today I only pressed snooze for fifteen minutes
even though I feel dead tired because I stayed up
marking essays and watching old episodes of *The West Wing*
and then I went to bed and looked at my phone and texted
a few of the long list of people I haven't replied to yet
with messages that start with something like
I'm so sorry! because that's how I have to start nearly every text

because today I want to drive out of the city
past Barlow and Unthank to Hathersage
to walk with Helen and take pictures of rocks and talk
about how we say sorry all the time and about all
the awful men we've apologised to as if we were the ones
who stalked or screwed or attacked or harassed
or undermined and it was not always the other way around
and I want to discuss lines like *I wanted to be near that burning.*
I still don't understand, but at least now my fingers ride the lip
that just stick their tips in your arms and knees and don't let go
and how that feels like a different of love

but before I do that I go to the toilet to check for blood
or at least a bit of pink or something
but there is still nothing there which is funny
but not *Haha* funny because now I'm three days late
and now my heart is beating a little bit faster
but I'm staying calm because this is No Big Deal
and because I'm playing a game where I see how long
I can not care and so I go to the other toilet
where I have one more test hidden in a tampon box
because it turns out I'm not that casual after all

and that after that scan last winter with that bruise
over my left ovary I keep thinking about this bag
of blood shadow inside of me and I can't help worry
that maybe I had my one chance when I was twenty-one
because how many times has that thought burrowed
into the shoes of everyone in the Marie Stopes waiting room

43

even when the people sitting with their hands in their laps
in those plastic chairs know what they are doing
is absolutely right or absolutely the only way
and so we sit with our shoes full of doubt and hate and fear
and certainty and eat our sandwiches and play Imagine
and think of future gynaecologists counting up our eggs
and guessing how many we've got left and then we taste fear
and get out our phones to play Snake instead

and so I am here six years later thinking of that room
with the five of us lying there on reclining chairs with tissues
and a glass of water and everything gone sniffing and texting
and waiting to stand up again and get picked up
when I fold the test up my pyjama sleeve and hold it
against my forearm the way I did at school and do at work
to shield friends and male co-workers from a tampon
and take it back and pee on it knowing that it'll be negative

  because I did a test three days ago that came back negative
and when I saw the single blue line put my trainers on and ran
as fast as I could around Hucknall and Mapperley and through
all the parks that everyone says you shouldn't go through at night
and up through the red-light street to the water treatment tower
that looks over the city because I needed to feel dangerous
and strong and indestructible even though when I got there
I sat on a bench in the dark and cried while I tried to catch
my breath but the shadows in my stomach wouldn't let me

and that night I went home and had a bath and cooked dinner
and played the No Big Deal game again but now here I am
three days later peeing on a new white stick
except that now my uterus and the scientists at ClearBlue
are playing their own game called Phantom and Crucifix
and now there are two blue lines and I stare
without blinking in case they disappear but they just keep on
proving and that ghost cross keeps rising up out of water
and the | is as strong as the – and I remember how last time
it only took seconds for the lines to appear and the leaflet
is just covering its tracks when it says two minutes and suddenly
I start to play a brand-new game called Risk + Secret

and everything is bright and terrifying because
I've got no knickers on and I'm going to drive to Hathersage

and I'm going to bury all of the shadows under a rock
and cover the spot with lichen to make them seem weathered
and done with and right now it's easy to count up shadows
and hide them under rocks and to play Risk + Secret

because it only seven twenty in the morning
and the forecast is clear until the afternoon
and it's another five hours and thirty-three minutes
before anyone is stabbed and shot in the street in Birstall
and because at that same moment forty-five miles away
we watch the climbers scale Stanage Edge and breathe up
places named Higgor Tor and the Dark Peak
which sound so aching and burying and knee deep
in unseen bog and up there playing games
eyes to the lip of the sky there is no need to look down
for the bad news.

File [3]

██████████ b. February 1899. Church of Scotland.
Unaccompanied. Second confinement.
Patient's spouse based overseas (Railways. East
India Co.). Unforthcoming
over the duration of his stay. Patient appearance:
blonde, high coloured, severely overweight.
Bloating of the hands and feet. Complains of
thirst and constant headache. Patient asserts
that she is six months gone. Foetus measures
large, unturned. Private room paid in full.
Adoption is already arranged.

[For the record: February, '20:
foetus delivered prematurely. Dead
upon arrival. Patient discharged after three days.]

File [4]

███████████ b. 1905(?) Dark hair
and eyes. Origin: unclear. Patient admitted
accompanied by officer. Feverish.
On close examination found to have
severe wound. Foreign

object found and removed. Discovered
at 73 Strathclyde Street after tip-off
from a Mrs P. Clarke, neighbour. Abortionist
arrested. Heavy bleeding. Thought to be
near due date. Patient unable to be
questioned. Sedated. Next of kin

still unlocated. [For the record:
December 1919. Patient and foetus
deceased. Listed cause of death: tuberculosis].

Now, Suture

                    leaves scars
smooth and neat like cable wire,
so the laddered track above your left wrist
betrays your age
                         (as does the way
the skin now has a memory of its own,
crêpeing when pinched only to fall away).
I run my finger to where the purple line
has bunched,
                    and feel silk snagged
in the two - pronged foot of the machine.

Its pucker,
                    and the way the corners itch
when it's about to snow
                              (think of
the ache of a phantom leg,
                                   or the herd
of cows that lie and wait upon their bellies
as the pressure falls)
                         says nothing
of what witchcraft might have hemmed
the pieces of your skin and bone
back together,
                    or what tore them
open first.

                    Prizing old wounds apart,
I glimpse your body in free fall,
                                   poised
between the garage roof and concrete floor:
the slow-motion playback of your radius,
jaunty,
          sharp,
                    as it breaks free from the bicep
and pierces a new window through
the epidermis;
                    hear the brittle crunch
of bone as it shatters.

                    Although we can
all marvel at the durability of children,
there must still be a sort of poignancy
in a trepanned arm,
                    a sadness held
in fingers that for two long hours
don't listen when they're told to bend.
I flinch to think of the cut telephone cord
and its fiddly re-wiring.
                        The tentative
current creeping,
                    then coursing
between your hand and the bundle of threads
tucked just beneath your skull.

It's only a playful trick though,
                            this little leap
between what's fact and what's pulled
out of the hat
                (I hardly look down
when I pick you up.)
                    and with luck
it'll be my arms
                    - almost as thin as yours -
searched for ugly marks.
                        Besides,
 it's always only the capacity of a verb
to crack,
        smash,
                splinter,
                        and then recast
that's really at stake.

Delivering

I already know
what it feels like

from watching the news;
I can feel in my aching pelvis

that it must be coming soon
not because I'm due

but because laws can break
as suddenly as waters.

It is never not the month
to labour

over what we tell our children
before they arrive

on boats, on top of trains, half
dead and rolling like matchsticks

in the back of transit vans,
slick and safe from our torn

and bleeding bodies.

Barely contained

I am admitting all of this
because of tenderness.

Did you know
that jellyfish are hardly
more than sea? *Water*
barely contained,
the biologist notes.

The moisture in the air
is dispersed
around this archive
through a complex set
of valves and pipes & fans,
each molecule slowly evaporating
until my face feels dry and taut
and breath lingers in the mouth.

Perfect preservation
calls for the right conditions.

The right air, the right pH,
the right tools - microfilm,
scales, index card, paper, gloves.

Portrait of a Pregnant Sonnet

Think of me not as a prison but as a beautiful house
where all the doors and windows are bolted

and everybody else has the key. I go to workshops
to meet editors who touch my body and tell me

I need to eat more words. I stay up late scrolling
message boards for signs that I'm laboured,

that the relationship between my form and content
is all wrong. At the sonnet class all the other sonnets

know how to behave. The perfect couplets sit in a circle
and smile at each other while I just keep saying to myself

that *opinions are like voltas, every body has one.*
But when I go swimming I submerge my feet and suddenly

I'm wordless. Free of syntax, Unformed. Diving under,
I roll my body over in a question mark, and exhale.

Emily Dickinson keeps writing me love letters

with tiny black peonies where each tittle should be
and exclamation marks at the end of every other sentence.

I am so excited! I am so sad! Emily Dickinson keeps declaring.
She writes long passages about the varying properties of roots

and then follows it with things like *my heart is made —
of ringing bells* and *we are a basket of herbs bound tight*

in God's twine! and I don't know what to think.
And all the while the dogs are outside

barking to be let back in and it hasn't stopped raining
in seventeen days. Each time I go to look up oscillation

another dried sprig falls out of the dictionary, and I remember
just how long there still is to go. Last week, when I opened

the kitchen window at least thirteen dead ladybirds fell
onto my hand, and if that isn't a sign then I don't know what is.

World

If you can still touch an empty stretch of sealskin,
or threaten to expose the holes between
each weave of copper wire

then go ahead and cradle the painted
ostrich egg blown hollow of its bird
and remember who it was that told you

that a world must be perfect,
which is all we really want, with our full moons,
our fear of cracks, our leap towards

the perfect orbit of the spinning skipping rope,
the pure black stones we pluck from the water
and circle in our palms all tell us

that spherical is right, that pi
can hold us and keep us warm,
but even perfect worlds must have their gore.

Deprived of their lines, continents can shift
into half rhyme, cross borders, spin and unwind
from no axis whatsoever. Even the equator can lie,

As mine does, splitting us to the right
of where we ought to join. At night,
I sit with my globe and feel for its hollows,

finding them in the tender countries
where we always meet, wait to feel each plate
give, knowing an imperfect world means pain.

But who was it that said that the world
must be perfect? World is no such thing.
Glorious and flawed, I lie in bed,

and when I turn the whole world rolls.
Watch now how a mountain range springs up
and just as easily dissolves.

Prescription

In her anthropological study, *Men and Mules*
Zora Neale Hurston notes down the way
to drive an unwanted person from the house.

When it is a man, she records, place his name
within the core of a sharp-headed onion
and roll it after him as he crosses the threshold
of the door.

         This year, I've seen it written
that stories, like viruses, are best spread
by word-of-mouth, how lore is just as prone
to mutate when threatened with containment.

See, we can fashion ourselves new metaphors
for the times and make them taste as bitter
as the black cat bone.

In her glossary of hoodoo, Hurston lists
the prescription for fistula:

sweet gum and mullen cooked down with lard.
Make a salve.
         Apply by hand.

     Throw an onion at the archive
and watch it roll and roll.

Note on *Speculum*

As the name suggests, this pamphlet is concerned with the body and the many tools employed to investigate within it; the steel or plastic surgical instrument inserted to examine the vagina and cervix, the held-held mirror, the ultrasound, the artist's charcoal, the writer's pen, the bare or gloved hand. All can illuminate and aid, all can exert power and violence over a woman laid bare from the waist down.

At its heart are the pieced-together histories of Anarcha, Lucy and Betsey, three enslaved women who were forced to undergo numerous experimental surgical procedures by the celebrated American doctor James Marion Sims - the so-called 'Father of Modern Gynaecology'. All of these operations were done without anaesthesia and without consent in what scholars such as Rachel Dudley have termed a 'medical plantation' - a cultural location of disability and a way of forcing enslaved women into another means of production by redefining the uses of their bodies.

Over a period of four years of experimentation, Sims invented the duck-billed speculum and gradually perfected the treatment for vesico-vaginal and recto-vaginal fistula — a procedure that he would go onto perform on wealthy and properly sedated women all over the world and an operation that has transformed and saved the lives of millions of women. He wrote extensively of these experiments - and through his papers gave glimpses of Anarcha, Lucy and Betsey. They come into blurred focus in letters and medical papers, as well as in his memoir *The Story of My Life*. The three women also appear in plantation ledgers and a census record from the time. Then, Sims leaves Alabama, and the women disappear from all record. Their lives, their experiences, their survival and their knowledge of midwifery and each other's bodies stops dead at the end of a sentence.

The painstaking work of historian Deirdre Cooper Owens has been fundamental to the conception of *Speculum*. her work shows how research, literature, and imagination can be tools to refuse this erasure. *Medical Bondage*, her ground-breaking study of the uncelebrated 'mothers of gynaecology', and its stunning use of archival material, was a driving force to finally begin writing on a subject and a set of intersections that have preoccupied me for over a decade, as well as to use my own archival training for a different purpose. Yet I unconsciously began *Speculum* long before I started writing anything resembling a poem down.

Five years ago, I started taking notes as my grandmother-in-law went through her six births. I wrote down dates and locations, fathers, hospitals, injuries, treatment. We talked about her bodily experiences of pregnancy and childbirth, first in Jamaica and then in London, and across our very different modes of talking about the body we found ways to whisper in crowded living rooms about sites of power; about violations and their retribution.

Fifteen years ago, I sat in another living room and listened as my own grandmother talked about her childhood and the discovery that her cold and distant sister was in fact her biological mother. She laid out everything she had been able to find about the circumstances of her birth on the floor in front of us. A few photocopied pages listing mother and baby homes from a Glasgow archive, yellowed photographs of a nondescript Victorian building, a single evasive letter from her brother-turned-uncle with small details of what he knew of the events of 1933 ('shipyard', 'gone', 'undisclosed', 'troubled'), polaroids of her birth mother, glamorous and drunk in 50s Brooklyn. The creation of this archive, and the complete nothingness of it, had consumed her for the entirety of her adult life.

My grandfather on the other hand, also adopted, refused to even discuss the circumstances of his birth. It was left to my grandmother to pass down the whispered conversations that she'd had with his adoptive mother fifty years before. Again, it was next to nothing. Only a few words ('disabled', 'teenager', 'abandoned', 'local').

Then four years ago I was pregnant with my daughter and profoundly sick and suddenly all the gender theory and archive theory and body theory and disability theory that I'd devoured as an academic tasted different in my mouth. It is as Sara Ahmed says, theory does more 'the closer it gets to the skin' (*Living a Feminist Life*, p.10). And all of the stories from friends and family and newspapers and history books and novels and letters and court proceedings and medical textbooks about women's bodies and the small and huge violences, violations, and mistreatments enacted upon, within, and against them talked to each other in a new way.

In her beautiful poem 'The Republic of Motherhood', Liz Berry steps across a bodily threshold into a new world. She begins: 'I crossed the border into the Republic of Motherhood | and found it a queendom, a wild queendom.' I, like so many others, found myself there too. And yet as I walked through its cemeteries and prayed to its ghosts ('Our Lady of the Birth Trauma, Our Lady of Psychosis'), I couldn't feel as exultant, or even as certain of who was in charge. These poems are an exploration of that uncertainty. They are also a new archive. They are as unfinished and as 'found' as the lives and deaths of the women in them. And, like the speculum, they are also a mirror.

Further reading

Alongside family records, this poetic archive drew heavily from material available in-person and online (a crucial benefit during 2020/21) at the Wellcome Collection in London. I only scratched the surface of the huge array of historical documents, images, objects and other material available to view. It is a remarkable collection. I am also grateful to the Foundling Museum and the Vagina Museum for their resources and records.

The poems directly and indirectly engage with a number of contemporary and historical texts, including:

Adjoa Andoh and Lynette Linton's production of *Richard II* at the Sam Wanamaker Playhouse, 2019.

Richard Barnett, *Crucial Interventions: An Illustrated treatise on the Principles and Practice of Nineteenth-Century Surgery*, (2015).

Susan Bordo, *Unbearable Weight: Feminism, Western Culture and the Body* (2003).

Patricia Hill Collins, *Black Feminist Thought* (1990, repr. 2000).

Deirdre Cooper Owens, *Medical Bondage: Race, Gender, and the Origins of American Gynaecology* (2017).

Charles Dickens, 'Received, a Blank Child', *Household Words* (1853).

Nora Doyle, *Maternal Bodies: Redefining Motherhood in Early America* (2018).

Rachel Dudley, 'Toward an Understanding of the 'Medical Plantation' as a Cultural Location of Disability', *Disability Studies Quarterly*, vol. 32, no.4 (2012).

Sharla M. Fett. *Working Cures: Healing, Health, and Power on Southern Slave Plantations* (2002).

William Hunter, *The Anatomy of the Human Gravid Uterus Exhibited in Figures* (1754).

Zora Neale Hurston, *Men and Mules* (1935).

Sarah Knott, *Mother: An Unconventional History*, (Penguin, 2019).

Jane Sharp, *The compleat midwife's companion: or, the art of midwifry improv'd. Directing child-bearing women how to order themselves in their conception, breeding, bearing, and nursing of children* (1724).

James Marion Sims, *The Story of My Life* (1888).

William Smellie, *A Treatise on the Theory and Practice of Midwifery (1752); A Sett of Anatomical Tables, with Explanations, and an Abridgement, of the Practice of Midwifery, (1754).*

Haworth, 1855. Charlotte Bronte died on the 31st March 1855. Although the cause of death was recorded as phthisis, it is more likely to have been as a result of Hyperemesis Gravidarum – acute morning sickness – or even as a result of refeeding syndrome.

Polish Aubaude. Stanisława Leszczyńska was a Polish midwife who was incarcerated at the Auschwitz concentration camp in April 1943. In the two years that she was imprisoned she delivered over 3,000 babies. Babies with blue eyes were taken away to be Germanized. The rest were either killed by the guards or other infirmary workers or died of starvation and exposure. It is believed that up to thirty children delivered by Leszczyńska did survive.

Person of the Year. In 2014 Salomé Karweh was named by *Time Magazine* as a Person of the Year for her frontline work fighting Ebola in West Africa. A survivor of the disease herself, Karweh later died in 2017 after delivering her son by caesarean section. She was left dying in her car outside the hospital for over three hours while doctors refused to touch her.

Statue. Fifteen-year-old Ann Lovett was discovered, along with her newborn son, in a grotto behind a statue of the Virgin Mary in Granard, County Longford, Ireland in 1984. Lovett had carried and delivered her child in secret. Both mother and child died.

Games. Jox Cox, the MP for Batley and Spen, was murdered by a right-wing extremist in Birstall on 16 June, 2016.

Acknowledgements and notes on poems

Thanks are due to the following publications in which some of these poems first appeared: *Poetry Birmingham Literary Journal, Into the Void, Bath Magg, Strix, Stand* and *Under the Radar*. 'Sorry' was published in *Verse Matters*, ed. Helen Mort and Rachel Bower', (Valley Press, 2017) and appeared on 'The Art of Apology', Radio 3, 2020. 'Haworth, 1855' won the YorkMix Poetry Prize in 2018. 'Juice' won the Newcastle Poetry Prize in 2019. 'World' and 'Delivering' have been translated into Arabic by Atef Alshaer and have appeared in *Al Arab*.

This collection owes a great deal to the NHS and its midwives, doctors, and staff. But it is primarily inspired by the countless anonymous women behind the official history of pregnancy, gynaecology and obstetrics. It is intended, in its very small and unfinished way, to offer an alternative poetic record.

Many friends have generously read, edited and encouraged these poems and their subject matter. Special thanks go to John Whale, Jon Glover, Elaine Glover, Helen Mort, Suna Afshan, Naush Sabah, Claire Pelly, Claire Protherough, Dana Ward, Emma Trott, Ragini Mohite, Rebecca Goss, Kim Bridger, Sophie Morley and Leila White for poetic, personal and medical advice and anecdote. I am also indebted to my past and present creative writing students and colleagues at the University of Westminster and Birkbeck. They are a constant source of inspiration and creativity.

Finally, thank you to Nick, my mother, my daughter, and the women in our lives, living and deceased, whose shared stories and experiences helped conceive of this hall of mirrors.

Last

... *to the hair's breadth*
to the still caught verb,
otter, minnow, thimble,
bone: know how I am
longing. Know that fear,
like an orange, is not
precisely sliced.

LAY OUT YOUR UNREST

Lightning Source UK Ltd.
Milton Keynes UK
UKHW022116210621
385910UK00003B/10